Zoom! How Cars Move

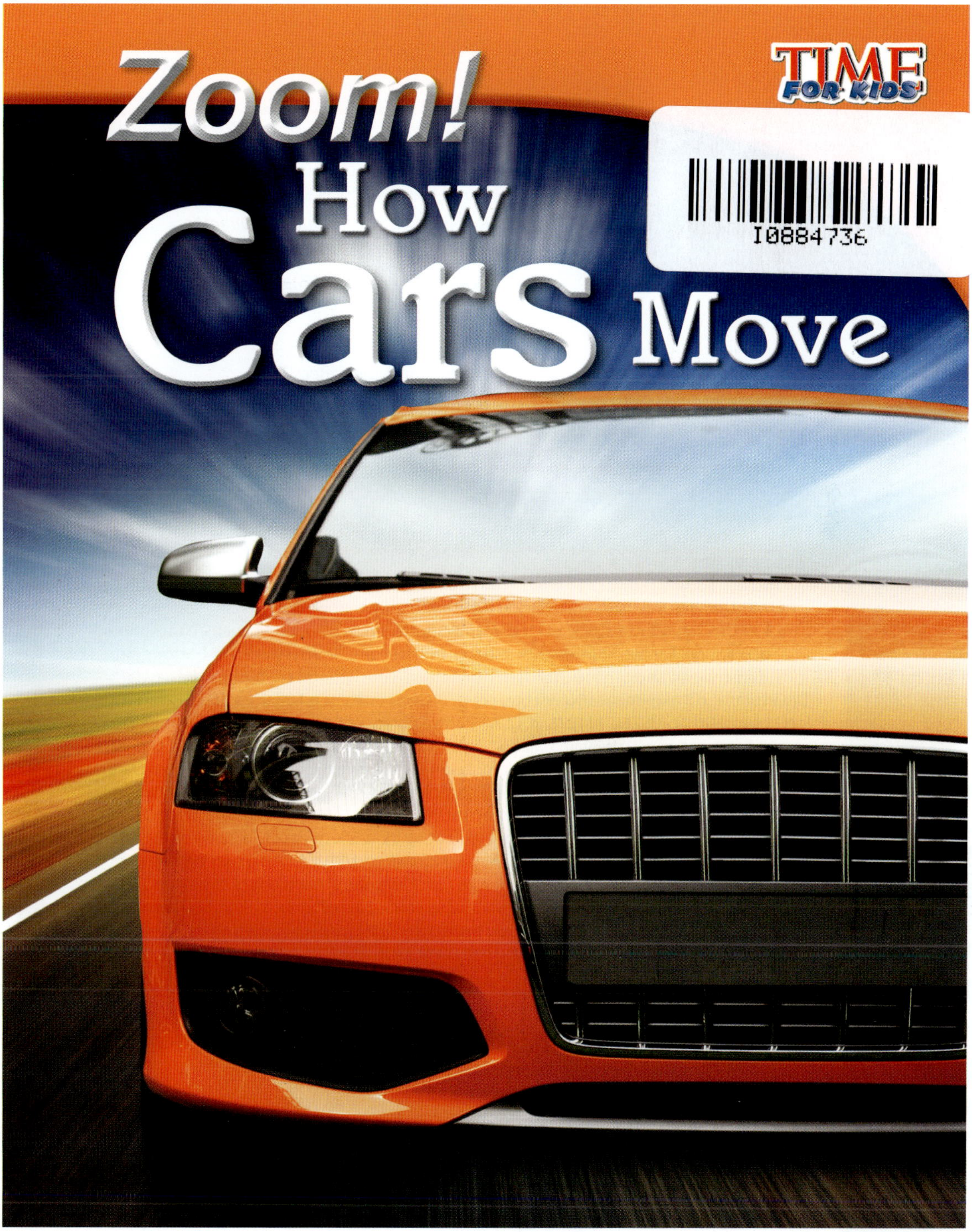

Jennifer Prior

Consultants

Timothy Rasinski, Ph.D
Kent State University

Alan J. Cross
Automotive Engineer

Publishing Credits

Dona Herweck Rice, *Editor-in-Chief*
Robin Erickson, *Production Director*
Lee Aucoin, *Creative Director*
Conni Medina, M.A.Ed., *Editorial Director*
Jamey Acosta, *Editor*
Heidi Kellenberger, *Editor*
Lexa Hoang, *Designer*
Stephanie Reid, *Photo Editor*
Rachelle Cracchiolo, M.S.Ed., *Publisher*

Image Credits

Cover Dudarev Mikhail/Shutterstock; ben smith/Shutterstock; p.3 Alex Mit/Shutterstock; p.4 Jordan Tan/Shutterstock; p.5 top: joyfull/shutterstock; p.5 inset: mevans/iStockphoto; p.5 caption: kanate/Shutterstock; p.6 top: michaeljung/Shutterstock; p.6 bottom: jan kranendonk/Shutterstock; p.7 top: kirin_photo/iStockphoto; p.7 bottom: Elegeyda/ Dreamstime; p.8 akg-images/Newscom; p.9 AFP/Getty Images; p.10 James Steidl/Shutterstock; p.11 top: LOC-LC-USZ62-111278; p.12 AP Photo/Library of Congress; p.13 top: Photolibrary; p.13 bottom: Kenneth William Caleno/Shutterstock; p.14 ArchMan/Shutterstock; p.15 top: Lutsan Pavlo/Shutterstock; p.15 bottom: Jason Swarr/Shutterstock; p.16-17 Andrea Danti/ Shuttertstock; ; p.18 elwynn/Shutterstock; p.19 top: Jess Yu/Shutterstock; p.19 bottom: dpa/ picture-alliance; p.20 gameanna/Shutterstock; p.20 inset: Alex Mit/Shutterstock; p.21 top: chungking/Shutterstock; p.21 bottom Igumnova Irina/Shutterstock; p.22 right: Calyx22/ Dreamstime; p.24 Tyler Olson/Shutterstock; p.25 top: o44/ZUMA Press; p.25 bottom: Paul J. Richards/AFP/Getty Images/Newscom; p.26 top: Photoshot/Newscom; p.26 bottom: Solent News/Splash News; p.28 James Steidl/Shutterstock; background: alekup/Shutterstock; 3DDock/Shutterstock; back cover: mevans/iStockphoto

Based on writing from *TIME For Kids.*

Teacher Created Materials
5301 Oceanus Drive
Huntington Beach, CA 92649-1030
http://www.tcmpub.com

ISBN 978-1-4333-3657-7

Printed in Malaysia
Thumbprints.42285

Table of Contents

Cars, Cars, Everywhere

Fast cars, race cars, cars that are slow,
Big cars, small cars, cars on the go,
Loud cars, quiet cars, cars that jerk and sputter,
When it comes to getting there, cars are like no other!

Automobile is another word for *car*.

Imagine life without cars. How long would it take to walk to the grocery store? How would you get the groceries home? How far away is the movie theater or the mall?

Cars make our lives easier. They keep us warm and dry as we travel in storms. We can travel long distances in a short time. How many places have you gone in a car this week?

Automobile History

In 1769, Nicolas Cugnot (koon-YOH) made a tractor for the French army. It used steam to move. It had three wheels and went just over two miles per hour.

Sometime between 1832 and 1839, Robert Anderson built the first electric **vehicle** (VEE-ih-kuhl). More electric vehicles were built throughout the 1800s and early 1900s. An electric car built in 1902 could go 14 miles per hour.

But, electric vehicles could not go very far. So, in 1876, Nicolaus Otto invented a gasoline engine that could. In 1885, Gottlieb (GOT-leeb) Daimler (DAHYM-lur) made the engine even better. Then Henry Ford helped make gas-powered cars the car of the future.

▼ Cugnot's steam vehicle

The Model T

In 1908, Henry Ford built a car called the *Model T*. Only one Model T was built at a time, so they were made very slowly. This made them expensive to buy. So, Ford thought of a different way to make them. He invented **assembly-line production**. That means a car is made by a line of people. Each person in line has a different job to do. They do the same work on every car. He also made the parts for each car the same size and shape, so the parts in one car would fit in another car, too. Cars could be made faster, and that saved money. With assembly lines, a basic Model T cost about $300.

▼ workers adding wheels to a car

Henry Ford tried many times to make the right car. He made Model A, Model B, Model C, and so on. Ford said, "Failure is only the opportunity to begin again more intelligently." After many tries, he finally made the Model T.

Have you ever seen a **carriage** that is pulled by a horse? That is a bit how the Model T looked. The Model T **roadster** could hold two people. It had no roof or doors. A roof and door were added to the Model T **coupe**. The **town car** was much the same, but it had a back seat, too. None of these cars had windshields or headlights. People had to pay extra to have them added!

Horseless Carriage

Before there were cars, there were carriages pulled by horses. When the first cars were made, people called them **horseless carriages**. That means they were like carriages, but with no horses.

Henry Ford (1863–1947) said, "Thinking is the hardest work there is." ▼

"So Long as It's Black"

Henry Ford is thought to have said that a customer could have a car in any color he or she wanted "so long as it's black." At first, Ford only made black cars. Later, color choices were added.

▲ 1908 Model T

In the early 1900s, few people dreamed of owning a car. They were expensive, and there were not enough roads. But, because of Henry Ford, more and more people were able to buy cars. Life was changed forever. Roads were built to connect cities. Cars could easily go from one place to another. People could go wherever they wanted to go. Cars gave people a new freedom.

A family in the 1920s goes for a drive. ▼

1940s car

1950s pickup truck

Automobile

The word *automobile* has two parts, *auto* and *mobile*. *Auto* means "self." *Mobile* means "moving." So an automobile is "self moving." It does not need horses to make it go. But it does need fuel!

How Car Engines Work

How does a car engine work? When you turn the key, the engine starts. In a gasoline-powered engine, the engine burns a mixture of gasoline and air. This kind of engine is called an **internal combustion engine**. Every minute, hundreds of small blasts happen inside. The blasts create energy. The energy causes the inside of the engine to **rotate**, which makes the car move.

Internal combustion engines need gas to make them go. ▼

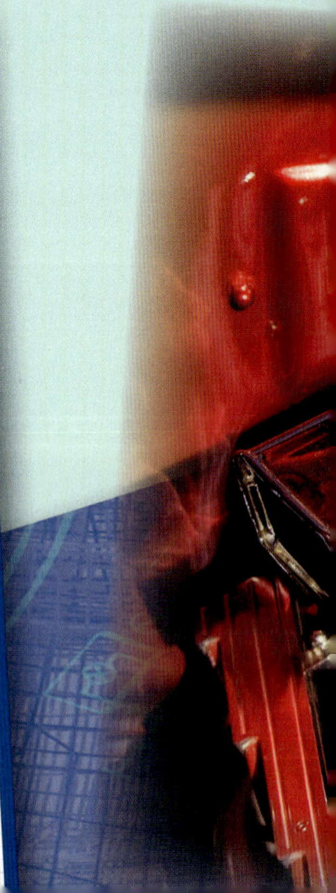

Gas Me Up!

Gas is the shortened name for **gasoline.** Gas is made from **petroleum** (puh-TROH-lee-uhm), so the British call it petrol.

internal combustion engine ▼ ▶

Combustion in Action

The **piston** starts in its cylinder. When the motor is cranked, the piston starts to move. When the cycle is completed, everything starts all over again and again, thousands of times. In a race car, it can happen more than 9,000 times per minute.

Inside the Combustion Engine

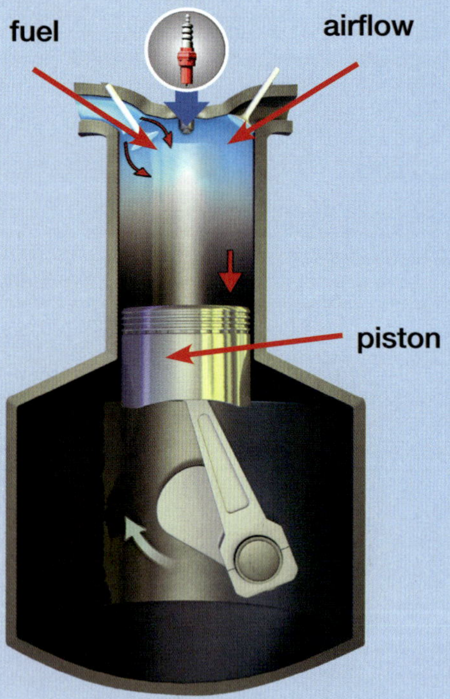

1. When the piston moves down, it lets the engine suck in a mixture of air and a tiny drop of fuel (gasoline) through the inlet valve.

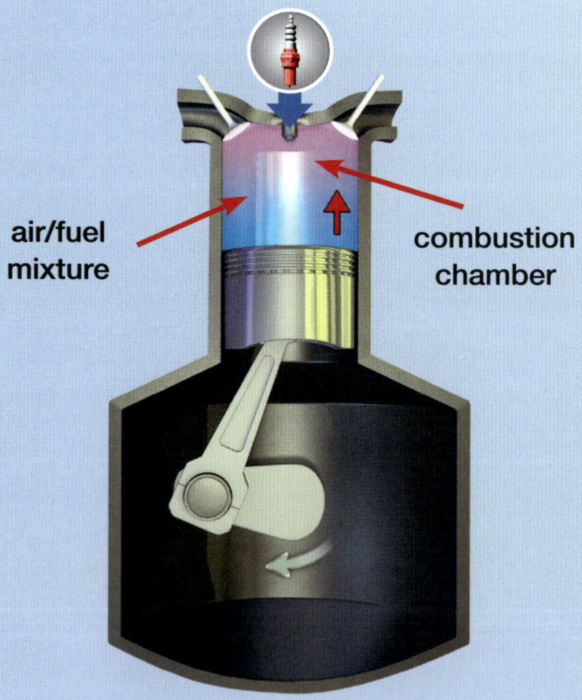

2. The piston goes back up, and the fuel and air mixture is **compressed** in the combustion chamber.

When airplanes were first invented, they used combustion engines, too.

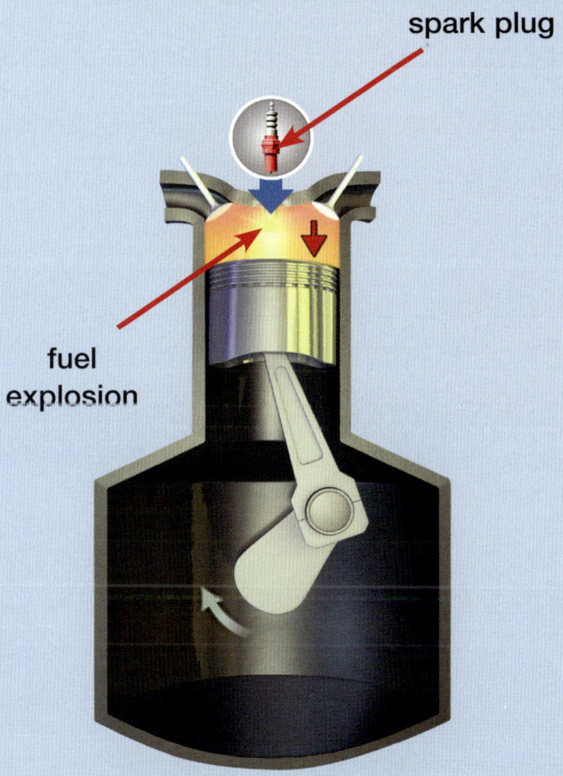

3. Next, the spark plug lets out a spark to light the fuel. There is an explosion, and the piston is forced down again.

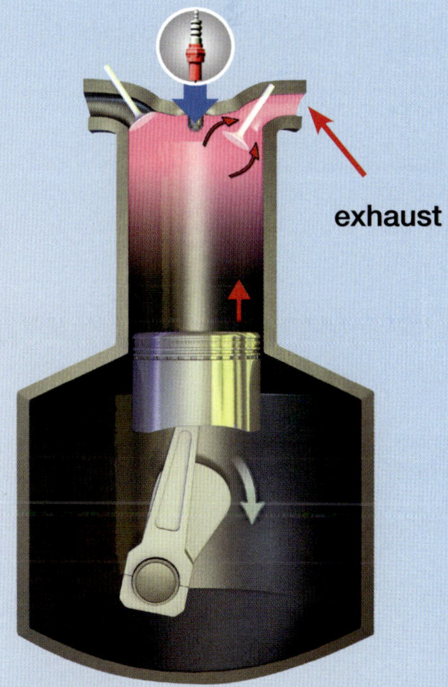

4. Finally, the **exhaust** is pushed out of the chamber and goes out the tailpipe of the car.

Pollution

A running engine creates exhaust. Exhaust fumes are **toxic** and unhealthy to breathe. With so many cars around, pollution is a problem. Have you ever seen smog? Much of it is caused by car engines.

People worry about the air. Polluted air is bad for living things. The government has made rules to protect the air. Engines must now create less air pollution. Fuel also burns "cleaner." This keeps the air clearer.

Automobile engines can create pollution in the sky. ▶

Clean Engines

Today, there are many types of clean engines being developed. Electric engines can go much farther than they could years ago. Natural-gas engines burn cleaner than most gas engines used today. **Hydrogen** (HI-druh-jehn) fuel cells convert the hydrogen gas to electricity without burning it, producing only water as a by-product. So, there is no pollution!

▲ Some cities have so much pollution that people must wear masks.

▼ car with an electric engine

Automobile Safety

Driving can be dangerous. A driver must get a license to drive. He or she must be careful to follow the rules of the road.

A driver needs to watch out for road **hazards.** Sometimes rocks are in the road. Sometimes there is roadwork. Children run into streets. Bad weather can cause problems, too.

Disc Brakes

Cars travel at high speeds. To make sure the vehicle stops safely, most cars today have disc brakes. The red "shoe" clamps onto the disc behind the tire and stops the wheel, using the force of friction.

Snow Safety

During winter, drivers may need to use chains or snow tires. Snow tires have an extra-deep groove in them that makes it easier to drive on the snow. Some drivers prefer to attach metal chains to the tires. This helps the car stay safe when driving through ice and snow.

A driver must use caution and drive slowly in bad weather. ▼

Most cars today are built for safety. Headlights help us see when driving at night. Seat belts hold us in our seats. In case of an accident, **air bags** protect people in the car. **Anti-lock brakes** help cars stop safely, especially in bad weather.

It is nice to have an easy way to get around. But we need to get to places safely.

How Seat Belts Work

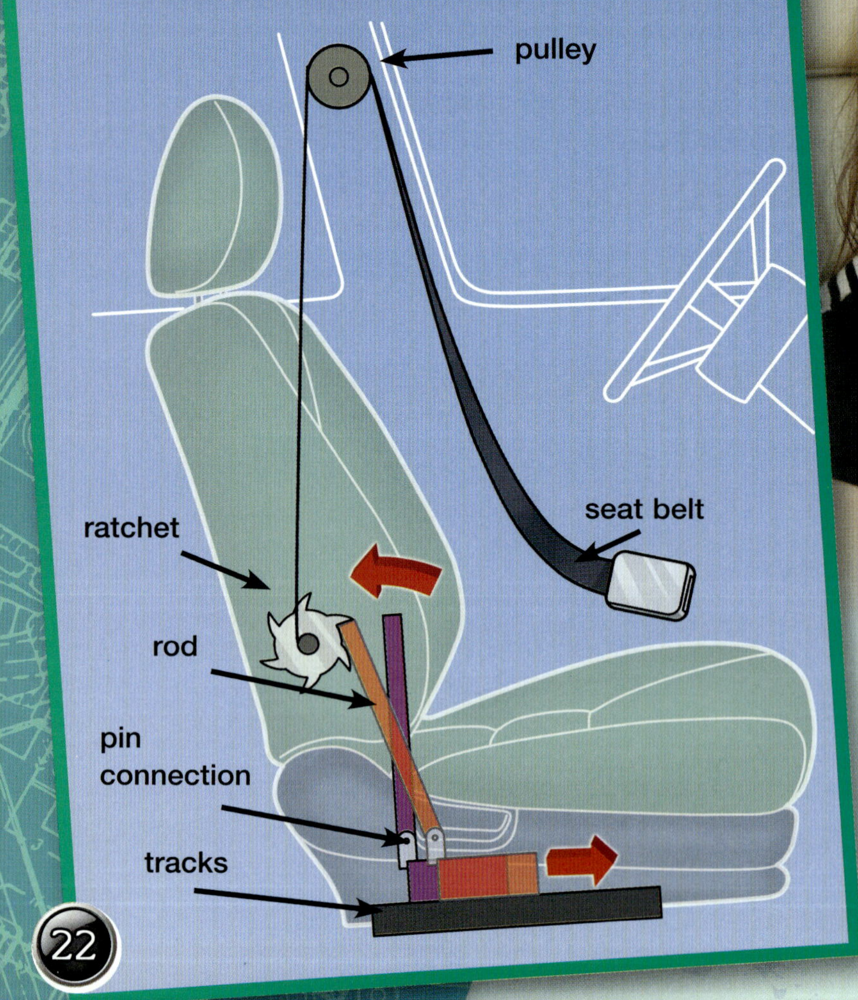

▲ It is important always to wear a seat belt.

In a car crash, the air bag may inflate. ▼

How Air Bags Work

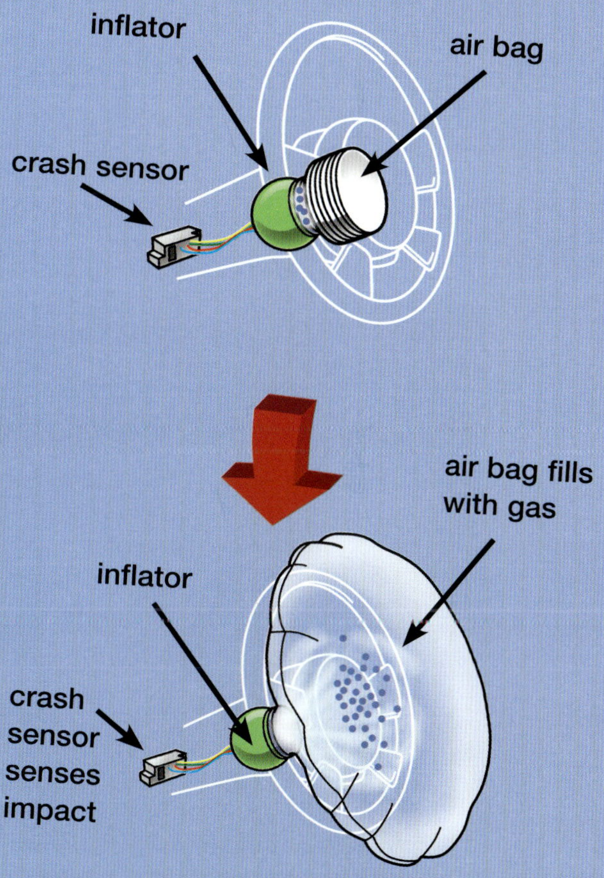

Today and Tomorrow

Cars have changed people's lives. Many people have jobs that depend on them. Some people build cars. Other people repair them.

Many people use cars to get to their jobs. They use them to run errands, to visit family and friends, and to travel. We even have drive-through restaurants and drive-in movies!

drive-through restaurant ▶

drive-in movie theater ▼

▲ ▼ possible cars of the future

Cars have changed a lot since the 1800s. Today cars continue to change. What new technology will change automobiles next?

Glossary

air bags—gas-inflated bags that protect drivers and passengers by inflating in an accident

anti-lock brakes—car brakes that do not lock up on slick roads, preventing cars from skidding out of control

assembly-line production—a way of making cars or other items so that the jobs are divided among many people; each person does the same job on each car (or other item) coming down the line

carriage—a cart, usually pulled by a horse, that carries people

compressed—to be pressed together tightly, usually into a smaller space

coupe—an enclosed two-door automobile

exhaust—poisonous fumes coming from a car into the air, released by small explosions of the car's fuel

gasoline—a fuel source for many cars

hazards—dangers

horseless carriage—a carriage run by power other than horses, such as steam, electricity, or gasoline

hydrogen—a colorless gas that is easy to ignite, is the lightest of all gases, and is the most abundant element in the universe

internal combustion engine—an engine that changes the force of an explosion into rotary motion (motion that goes around)

petroleum—an oily substance that gasoline is made from

piston—a metal piece used to create combustion

roadster—a small, open car with one seat for two or three people and a rumble seat (seat that opens from the back of a car) or luggage compartment in the back

rotate—to spin in a circle, around and around

town car—a large four-door sedan

toxic—poisonous; very harmful to living things

vehicle—something used to carry people, animals, or things, especially across land

Index